I NEED

By Green Fig Team

Green Fig
Proud Muslim Kids

Design by CHY

CHY Illustration & Design

Name:

....

Publisher: Green Fig
Pennsylvania, USA
www.gogreenfig.com
info@gogreenfig.com

Green Fig

Teach Me How To Pray - First edition
Paperback ISBN: 978-1953836717

DEAR PARENTS AND EDUCATORS,

I Need is a heartfelt book crafted to introduce young children to the concept of reliance on God. Through simple and relatable sentences, it highlights the basic needs we all depend on—air, water, family, and love—while gently connecting these blessings to to the ultimate truth: God is the Provider of everything.

In the Qur'an, Allāh says in Surat Al-Ikhlas ﴾اللَّهُ الصَّمَدُ﴿ which means, "Allāh does not need anything and everything needs Allāh." Allāh says in Surat Āl-Imrān, ﴾فَإِنَّ اللَّهَ غَنِيٌّ عَنِ الْعَالَمِينَ﴿ Which means, "Indeed, Allāh is free of need from the worlds."

This book encourages children to reflect on their many blessings and to understand that while we need many things, most of all, we need God, the Creator and Sustainer of all. Unlike us, Allāh is free from all needs.

We hope **I Need** sparks meaningful conversations and inspire young readers to develop gratitude, faith, and a deeper knowledge of their Creator.

With blessings,
Greenfig Team

I need a place to live.

I need clothes

6

to wear.

I need

8

air to breathe.

9

I need water to drink.

I need **food** to eat.

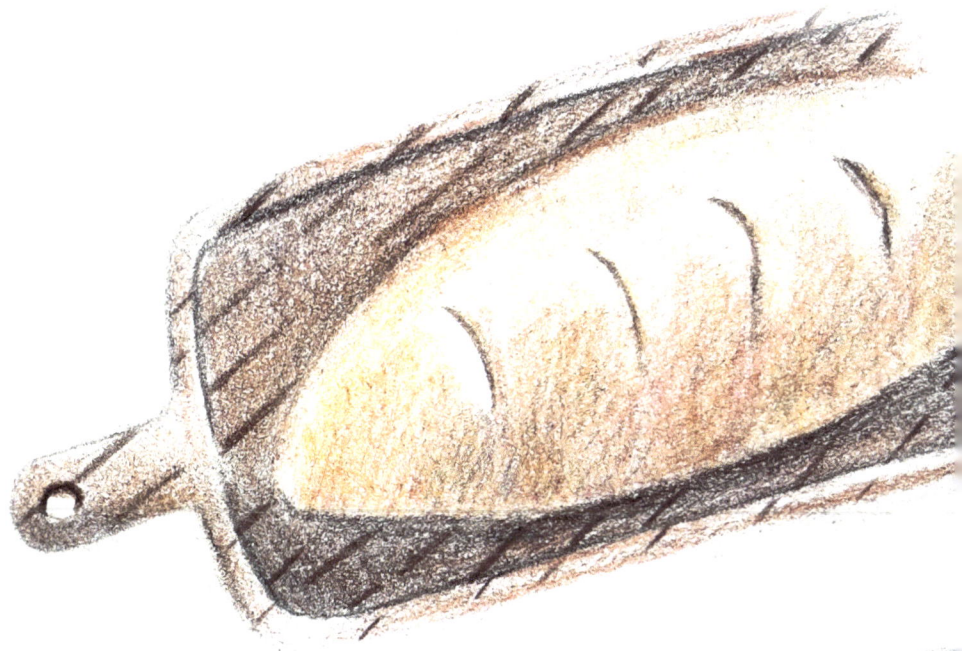

13

I need love

to feel secure.

I need

feet to walk.

I need **hands** to feel.

Tweet   Tweet

Tweet

Tweet

I need ears to hear.

21

I need eyes to see.

I need to **rest** sometimes.

24

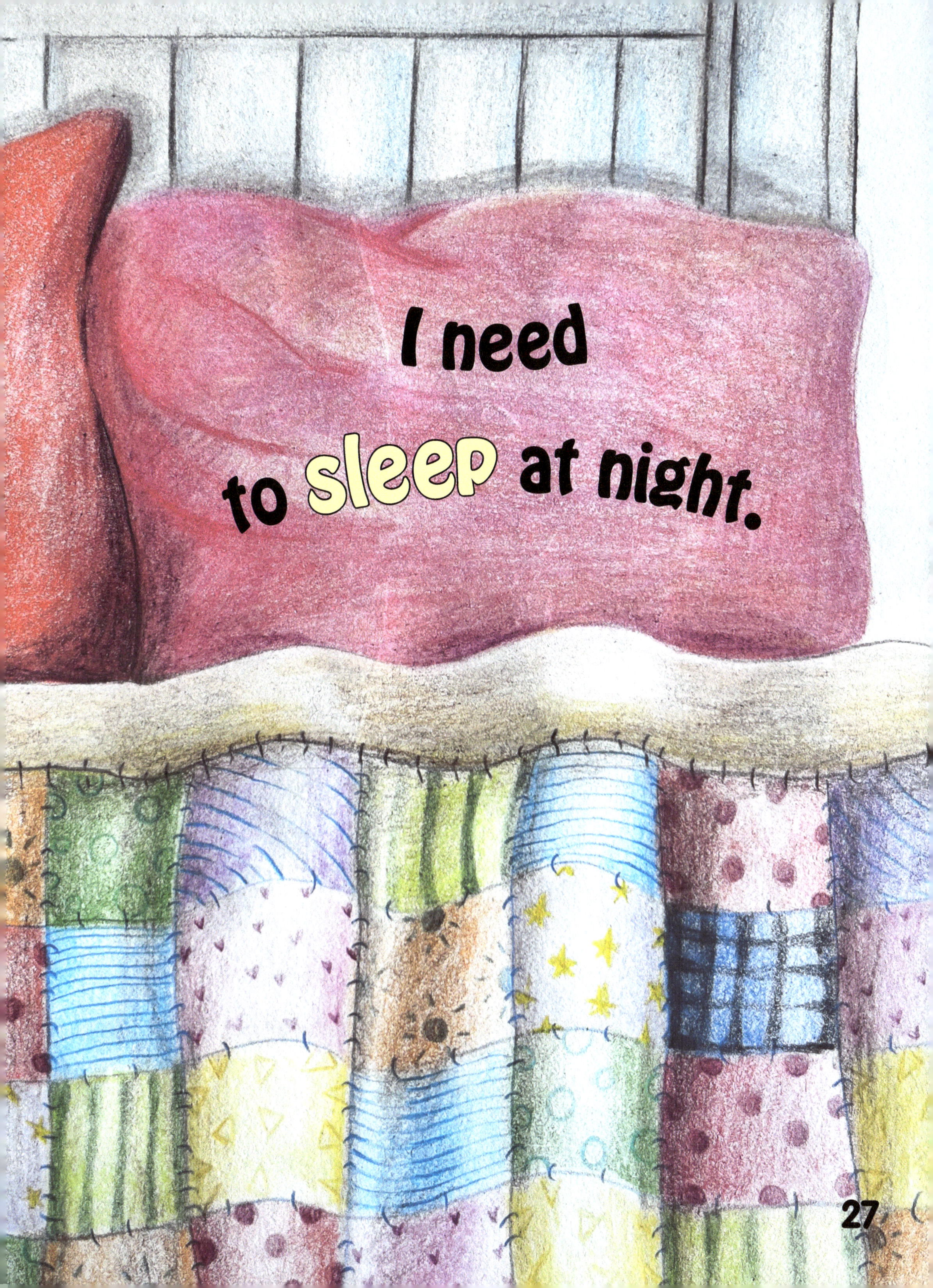
I need
to sleep at night.

I need **God** all the time. But

God does not need anything